THE ART AND SCIENCE OF LIFE

ISBN: 978-0-6397-3113-1

THE ART AND SCIENCE OF LIFE

UNDERSTANDING HOW FUNCTION AFFECTS OUR FUTURE

CHRISTINA ANDRIANATOS

INDEX

DEDICATION

This book is dedicated to my father, whose passion however different to my own, has inspired me throughout my life in following my heart, going for what I believe in and the pursuit of true value in life.

A NOTE FROM THE AUTHOR

This book was written with the intention of helping, informing and inspiring those who could benefit from the information and guidance within. It is a perspective on life and how certain actions can assist us in our journey to live more productively, healthily and happily.

This book is for the average person to be able to understand that the principles of a healthy mind and healthy body will lead to a healthy life. It is not a substitute for medical attention but rather a book to show how the body and mind are related, how this affects our everyday lives and how we can use the information herein to benefit ourselves by becoming aware of our bodies, minds and how they work in order to live healthier, more productive lives. It is a cognitive behaviourist approach to inspire positive change and awareness. By sharing the knowledge and research of how our bodies relate to our minds, to our emotions and, in turn, to how we perceive the world, how we react and respond to the world and to others; we can take control and responsibility of ourselves in order to make necessary changes for our futures.

The principles and ideas related in this book can be used by anyone, throughout life, in any situation and as a guide for better living, relationships and values.

To start off I will leave you with the following two quotes to consider.

The life of wisdom must be a life of contemplation combined with action. It is required to go beyond the idiosyncratic and egocentric perception of immediate experience. Mature awareness is possible only when I have digested, comprehended and compensated for the biases and prejudices that are the residue of my personal history. Each time I approach a strange object, person or event, I have a tendency to let my present needs, expectation or past experiences determine what I will see.

If I am to appreciate the uniqueness of any datum, I must be sufficiently aware of my preconceived ideas and characteristic emotional distortions.

- DR M. Scott Peck

Wisdom is not about having all the answers; it is often about asking the right questions.

Information is never just information. It is what we interpret into it, which depends on our context.

- DR Christian Busch

INTRODUCTION

Are we not carefully constructed beings, refined from each and every experience and our responses to our experiences? Are we carefully and precisely created with the ability to determine the results of our future by how we respond to life's experiences, or are we just the result of our behaviours and experiences with no control over how we are affected?

How can our actions or reactions change our entire life and future? How powerful are our perspectives and perceptions of our lives, our environment and those around us? Can a simple change in these cause our lives to transform into a completely different path/outcome and way of thinking in our journey? At times, a sudden trauma or enlightening moment or even something simple in everyday life can trigger an emotional and motivating response to our current circumstances which suddenly changes our perspectives and mindset. Where we once conformed to familiar social and environmental customs, belief systems or ideals, we suddenly realise that we are not satisfied with the current outcomes and circumstances of our lives and want more. Many more times than not, this starts from a single small action or reaction. It may be as simple as a conversation, hearing a song or reading an article. Something clicks inside our minds to create that AHA! moment! Something simple that leads to much larger transformations, that leads to better relationships or professions, that can start the process towards a lifestyle change where we live healthier, more fulfilling lives or reach previously unreachable goals. This book is about change, why change is necessary in order for us to evolve and how our behaviours are linked and usually are the cause of how we feel about life and our circumstances.

It is about the unconscious ideals and beliefs that sometimes restrict us from living the lives we truly wish to live; it is about understanding the cognitive reactions, behaviours and biases influencing us daily, and how we can use all of this to our advantage to change our lives around for the better.

This book, in its entirety, is about taking control of our lives, taking responsibility for our actions and beliefs, and using them to our own benefit. It is how, by understanding how our body functions and processes information, and how by using our senses and our behavioural responses, we can change our perspectives and perception in order to live a healthier and more fulfilling life by making better choices and having a clearer mindset of how to deal and respond to life. Empowerment in life can only be achieved through taking full responsibility for our lives.

CHAPTER ONE
BODY FUNCTION

You can be fully in charge of your life only if you can acknowledge the reality of your body, in all its visceral dimensions.

- Elvin Semrad

A simplified and brief overview of body parts, function and behaviour in relation to our daily lives.

The body is an incredible thing, magnificent really, in its ability to rewire itself, to grow and to adjust, all while we go about our daily lives, oblivious to all the incredible feats our bodies undertake in order to survive. Most times, unless we are ill or injured, we will not notice anything regarding our bodies and how they function. Until something is not working properly or how we feel it should be functioning, it usually gets taken for granted. We wake up with the expectation that everything will function correctly and focus on our surroundings, relationships and interests without a second thought as to how our bodies are coping. That is until we don't feel well or we notice a change in our bodies. Is this why stress and anxiety impact us in such an intense way? We automatically presume that we can cope with anything and everything; we live unhealthy lifestyles with the expectancy that our bodies will manage as if we were the healthiest and most health-conscious beings out there. So when stress and its characteristics start showing up, we ignore them and assume that they will go away, all while they start to accumulate and take their toll on our bodies. Our health starts failing; our mental state starts spiralling into a panic and suddenly we are falling apart and unable to cope. It happened out of nowhere... or did it? Usually, this deterioration results from long periods of unhealthy habits and lifestyle choices that go unchecked or are avoided or misunderstood.

Understanding the body and how it works has significantly positive benefits. When we understand how our bodies and minds are connected, we can see how noticing changes in our body can alert us to mental issues and stress. By understanding that our emotions and mental state can deeply impact our physical state, we can learn to take better care of ourselves in order to live healthier, more productive lives.

THE MIND

/mʌɪnd/

noun

1. the element of a person that enables them to be aware of the world and their experiences, to think, and to feel; the faculty of consciousness and thought.
2. a person's ability to think and reason; the intellect.

- Oxford Languages

One of the greatest questions that can be asked is: What is the mind? This leads to many other questions with varying neurological and psychiatric disorders. The hypothalamus is responsible for controlling our hormones and directly influencing our autonomic nervous system. It maintains our internal balance, and it plays a significant role in maintaining our physiological state, and regulating our emotional state and temperature, and plays a role in our sexual arousal. The pituitary gland produces and discharges the hormones which control our metabolism, growth, sexual maturation and blood pressure. The cerebellum is responsible for our balance and movement, while the prefrontal cortex plays an important role in our cognitive control functions. By doing so it enables and manages our attention, prospective memory, inhibition, cognitive flexibility, impulse-control, problem-solving, and comprehension and plays an important role in our creativity and reasoning abilities. The brain stem regulates our physiological state, the medulla controls the regulation of our heartbeat and breathing, while the thalamus takes information back and forth between the cerebral cortex and the senses.

Let's look at a few of these and other body parts in slightly more detail to gain a better understanding.

CENTRAL NERVOUS SYSTEM

The nervous system is made up of two systems: the central nervous system and the peripheral nervous system. The central nervous system is comprised of neurons making up the brain and the spinal cord. The peripheral nervous system is comprised of the motor peripheral system and the sensory peripheral system. Its main function is to collect, interpret, store, process and integrate the information coming in. The peripheral nervous system takes the information from the periphery to the central nervous system, which then uses the information to coordinate the processes and response our body makes to the information.

THE SENSORY PERIPHERAL SYSTEM

The sensory peripheral system is made up of two parts, the special senses and the general sensations. The difference between these is that special senses are senses generated from a specific part of the body and general sensations, being that they are generated from many parts. For example, your eyes generate special senses as you are only able to see from your eyes and no other part of your body; whereas with the sense of touch, you can feel this from many body parts. An example of both special and general sensory sensation would be that of the tongue, where tasting is a specific and special sense; whilst touching your tongue with your finger would be a general sense.

NEURONS

The nervous system is made up of two types of cells: the neuron and the glial. Neurons are conducting cells and glial cells are classified as non-conducive cells. Neurons send and receive signals; they send electrical pulses and are defined by function as well as type. The types of neurons are: unipolar, bipolar or multipolar and are defined by how many processes they facilitate. One singular neuron is capable of receiving information from thousands of surrounding neurons.

The information gathered from the periphery is transported through the spinal cord to the brain, which then processes the information. Neurons (nerve cells) produce the physical actions and responses. Their function is the communication of information throughout the body.

There are three functional types of neurons: the efferent (motor) neurons, the afferent (sensory) neurons and the interneurons (associative). Let's look at what each type of neuron does in order to understand the process as a whole.

The efferent neurons carry the information from the brain to the periphery, while the afferent neurons bring information from the senses to the brain. This is all connected by the interneurons which connect the efferent and afferent neurons by relaying the information between them and to the central nervous system. Approximately 99% of the neurons in our body being interneurons.

Each neuron is made up of three parts: the cell body, the dendrite and the axon. Active neurons send an electrical pulse down the axon, which reaches the synapse and communicates with another cell through its dendrite. The process of passing electrical impulses from one cell to another is called action potentials. These cause what is known as neurotransmitters (a release of chemical substances) and are passed on to the next cell. White matter (axons and ancillary cells) surrounds the neurons which link both the left and right hemispheres.

Grey matter is the cell bodies of neurons inside the central nervous system, while white matter is the axons as a collective within the central nervous system.

Nerves are the collection of axons outside of the central nervous system. Neuroplasticity is the body's ability to re-wire itself and find a way to perform the same function, yet in a different way. In this way, it is able to function despite damage. The brain has the ability to re-wire or fix itself, creating new neural networks in order to keep functioning.

MIRROR NEURONS

"Mirror neurons are one of the most important discoveries in the last decade of neuroscience. These are a variety of visuospatial neurons which fundamentally indicate human social interaction. Essentially, mirror neurons respond to actions that we observe in others. The interesting part is that mirror neurons fire in the same way as when we actually recreate that action ourselves. Apart from imitation, they are responsible for a myriad of other sophisticated human behaviour and thought processes. Defects in the mirror neuron system are being linked to disorders like autism."

- Acharya S & Shukla S. (2012). P.118 Mirror neurons: Enigma of the metaphysical Modular brain. Journal of Natural Sciences and Biological Medicine. 3(2):118-24.

Let's look at this a bit further; have you ever been sitting somewhere minding your own business, having a coffee or chatting to a friend when you start to feel as though someone is watching you? You feel someone's gaze directly on you even though they are not in your direct line of vision. When you turn around, to discover that there is in fact, someone looking at you! While you may feel proud of your psychic abilities, these are in fact your mirror neurons activating a response to your environment from the sensory input your body is receiving. These neurons activate purposely when an action can be identified by its purpose.

"When you know the intention behind an action, a different system in your brain is activated, involving the mirror neurons. That ability to understand the sensory implications; that is what you're going to see, of the motor actions you're perceiving allows you to create a map in the mind, if you will, that's correlated with neural firing patterns in this mirror neuron superior temporal area complex, that creates a neural representation, a neural map, of my intention in your head. In other words, beyond just seeing behaviour, we see the intention beneath the behaviour from the very beginning."

- Dr Dan Siegel - www.psychalive.org

THE PRIMARY VESICLES

The three primary vesicles are the forebrain, midbrain and hindbrain or prosencephalon, mesencephalon and rhomboncephalon.

The outer part is called the telencephalon (cerebrum), which contains the cerebral hemispheres, and the inner part is the diencephalon. The diencephalon houses the thalamus, hypothalamus, epithalamus and subthalamus. Diencephalon is a part of the forebrain (prosencephalon), just above the midbrain (mesencephalon) and is covered by the telencephalon on its sides. It is important to note that the optic nerves are not true nerves, but rather a part of the central nervous system derived from the diencephalon.

OCCIPITAL COMPLEX

The cerebrum is known for having two hemispheres, the left and right, which are then each divided up into four sections called lobes. The four types of lobes are the occipital lobes, the frontal lobes, the parietal lobes and the temporal lobes.

The occipital lobes are responsible for the translation of visual data, and each work by controlling the opposite visual field. The two systems which result are vision for perception and vision in action. The first helps to recognise objects and form a foundation base of knowledge; the second system enables you to interact with objects and with your movement.

The frontal lobes are responsible for our voluntary movement, cognition, and language.

The parietal lobes are responsible for the processing of sensory information.

The temporal lobes are responsible for our hearing and our interpretation of sounds into what we can understand; they are also responsible for formation of our memory.

Damage to certain parts can cause serious defects in our behaviour, and it has been noted that certain individuals who have had damage to the Broca's area of the cerebral cortex can suffer from Aphasia or loss of speech.

THE THALAMUS, HYPOTHALAMUS, PREFRONTAL CORTEX AND RELATED FUNCTIONS

The medial thalamus adjusts your psychological and physical state according to your mood. If you are emotionally affected, you will be more likely to remember that which you have experienced. So, the medial thalamus constantly adjusts your emotional state based on the sensory information you are experiencing (all except olfactory). The prefrontal lobe is specifically involved with your behaviour, thoughts, thinking processes and personality. There is a two-way connection between the medial thalamus and the prefrontal cortex. Sensory information, motor centres and thinking centres information is collected by the basal ganglia and dorsal medial nucleus in the thalamus and then your mood is adjusted accordingly. For example: if you are watching a funny movie, you will feel happy; if you are inside and feeling warm because your temperature is at the right level, you will feel comfortable. The same is said for bad feelings. Your body will adjust its emotional state based on the sensory information coming in, which causes you to have a more negative emotional state. The frontal lobe, covered by the prefrontal cortex, is primarily responsible for our thoughts, and the thalamus is what controls and regulates the information which it receives.

The visual primary cortex (area 17) is responsible for visual stimuli. The visual stimuli is then projected to the secondary cortex (area 18) where it is analysed and then further onto the tertiary cortex (area 19) where it will be compared to past experiences in order to be understood. For example, you are looking at a car, and in the secondary cortex, you will analyse what colour the car is, the size of the car, whether it is matte or shiny, it is new or old and so on.Then in the tertiary cortex; you will compare the car to a car you have seen previously, allowing recognition or not.

The same is said for the other senses: for touch, the somatic sensory areas do the same process of processing the stimuli received by the body in order to understand it.

Damage to these can cause difficulty or inability to understand the stimuli being received or sensory aphasia, for example: the inability to understand a language that was once understood.

The hypothalamus had three functions: it is related to the limbic system, it is related to the autonomic nervous system and it has an important influence on the endocrine system. It is related to many body functions, but we will just cover a few of interest.

In the hypothalamus, there are three parts which regulate hunger and satiety: the lateral hypothalamic area, the arcuate nucleus and the ventromedial nuclei. The ventromedial nuclei is responsible for our feeling of fullness (satiety) when it is stimulated; without it being stimulated, you would still feel hungry and keep eating. When stimulated, the same area (the same nucleus and neurons) enable you to feel happy. When you are hungry, you can feel agitated or angry, and when you are full, you can feel content and happy.

There are links between the responsible neurons in the hypothalamus. When affected by damage or tumours, it can cause overeating or under-eating, which can affect our mood and emotions. Hypothalamic injury can cause serious problems which affect a variety of processes and functions in the body. Thus, you can describe the ventromedial centre as the part which is responsible for the related positive-affecting emotions and the dorsalmedial nucleus for the related negative-affecting emotions. The lateral hypothalamus and dorsalmedial nucleus usually function at the same time, meaning that hunger and anger are the functions of the lateral hypothalamus and also the dorsalmedial nucleus.

Happiness, pleasure and satiety are functions of the ventromedial nucleus. If the dorsalmedial nucleus is overstimulated you will behave in a wild and unruly way. If both dorsalmedial nuclei are damaged you would become passive.

THE VISUAL PROCESS

..."the mind is the real instrument of sight and observation, the eyes act as a sort of vessel receiving and transmitting the visible portion of the consciousness".

Pliney the Elder: The Natural History

Visual stimuli that are transformed into imagery which we then recognise, are first processed from the retina. The results are sent via the optic nerves in the back of the eye, with signals being transported from one side of the visual field to the opposite hemisphere. They are transported through the geniculate nucleus and reach the cortex. Other secondary routes are responsible for controlling eye movement and registering day and night.

Through constant movement, the eye searches for information in its visual field. The eye does more than just transmit an accurate copy of the light distribution on its receptors; it transmits information to the brain which has already been highly interpreted.

VISUAL PERCEPTION

The retina converts signals;however, we all have what is known as a "blindspot", which is the part of the eye where there are no photo receptors to convert light. The visual cortex replaces this missing segment with what it perceives to be appropriate, consequently, what you are seeing may not actually be the true image. It is generally quite accurate, but there are times when what we think we see is not an accurate depiction of what is in front of us, due to our mind editing and filling in the blank "blindspot" and thus creating a visual illusion.

Our brains constantly process the information from our visual perceptions and then define and give it meaning by what is called internal representation. As such, even after we have seen what is in front of us and our mind may have altered the information, it once again gives its own definition and idea of what the information is and how it can be used once it reaches our brain.

There are people who suffer from various problems related to vision, including prosopagnosia (the inability to recognise faces), aphantasia (the inability to create mental imagery) and some of these can help or hinder us from being able to understand certain easily achievable or understandable behaviours and actions in everyday life. Imagine, for example, that you were unable to create mental images in your mind, which is something that is often used when planning or visualising a goal. It is how many sports coaches and therapists help their clients to visualise their end result and/ or a positive perspective of a situation. If you were unable to form and create mental imagery in your mind, would this not make this much more difficult, and more complicated to understand?

If you were unable to recognise people, no matter how many times you met them, would that not be frustrating and make things complicated for you on an everyday level? It is something that most people would take for granted as an automatic ability. Now most people will not suffer from anything like this, however, they will still be receiving information from their environment based on their sensory inputs.

When we use visualisation processes, we activate the same neurons in our secondary motor cortex as when we are doing the action for real. This is called signal flow. Simulation training is a method used by many coaches in areas such as sports and athletics, where an athlete or individual can prepare themselves. By doing this, the brain acts in the same way as if the individual was actually doing the action. Neurons can activate just by seeing an image of the action.

Individual neurons respond to the characteristics of faces, and not to specific faces, reducing recognition to the geometry of the facial measurements, according to Jon Turney in his book, Cracking Neuroscience.

For example, I found this especially interesting as an artist, as when I draw portraits, I start the drawing by outlining specific key shapes of the individual's face. If you are an artist or know any, you will know that most artists do not start this way but in fact, begin by drawing from a certain starting point (such as an eye or a mouth) and draw based on visualisation or copying what they are looking at in front of them or from an image.

I draw each basic shape first from an image, then add all the details, and then connect the entire drawing together with different shades of dark and light. This is not the usual or "correct" way to draw, according to artistic teachings; however, my drawings are still accurate as realistic portraits. I'm sure there are others who use this method out there as well.

Clearly my brain is unconsciously using the same technique it does for registering facial geometry to form and recognise a face in the way I am drawing and creating faces out on pen and paper. I found that my "own way" of drawing was more accurate and easy to follow than trying to draw by traditionally taught methods.However, what I was really doing was using the same techniques used by my mind on a daily basis of processing and recognising the faces of people around me. Unconsciously my mind connected the two, and my body was able to use this process in different ways; the mind understood the process and automatically associated it and used the same method with which it was familiar.

THE OLFACTORY SYSTEM

Molecules transported to the back of the nose activate cells that pass information via the cranial nerve fibres past the olfactory bulb and the thalamus directly to the hippocampus and amygdala - the brain regions which rouse emotion.

Have you ever had an emotional response to a certain smell? Have you ever been brought back to a memory of a place or person just from a certain scent? Does this affect how you react in a new situation based on your past feelings about that previous experience?

Of course.

If you are brought back to a happy memory, you will feel good and react in a very different way than you would if you were reminded of a terrifying or upsetting situation. You may avoid the smell completely, or not want anything to do with the new situation at all, based purely on the feelings experienced when being reminded of the past. Imagine you smell a scent which reminds you of an attacker; it would bring about fear, anger or many other emotional memories for you. The scent may not have anything to do with the new situation, besides what you are making of it. It could be that the person you are speaking to is wearing the same perfume as the person who attacked you did. Would you trust this new person while feeling all these mixed emotions? Would they affect your rational thinking of what to do in the new situation? Would you be able to concentrate without being emotionally affected?

On the other hand, think of someone you love dearly; if you met someone new and they wore the same perfume as the person in your mind, would you feel an automatic connection with them? Would you feel more trusting and comfortable with them? The answer is most likely yes; nine times out of ten, we do not realise it. Many times we do not realise the scent which is reminding us of previous experiences is even there, especially if it is a positive one and we are not being led through horrific memories. It may be that the scent is held in our subconscious, and we have not realised it has any effect on us at all.

This can be said for many of our sensory reactions and our cognitive responses to situations.

HORMONES

The endocrine system, controlled by the hypothalamus, is responsible for many functions, including our metabolism, our growth and sexual development and our moods.

An important hormone, which many of us know, is adrenaline. This hormone is released in preparation for our "fight or flight" reaction. Our body reacts to threatening situations in a number of ways. We feel a change in temperature or even break out into a cold sweat, our hearts start racing, we feel an energy surge, or we feel shaky and dizzy, and blood is diverted from the stomach to the muscles. There are many different reactions which depend on the situation and our emotional response to it. Once the situation has passed, it's possible to still feel these symptoms for awhile after as the response remains. Think of a stressful situation you have experienced before - how did you feel and how did you feel after the event? Many people find that even after an event has passed or whenever they think of the event or memory, they feel the same symptoms as if they are still experiencing the situation in real-time.

Many individuals, who have experienced trauma, find that there are all sorts of triggers from daily life which take them straight back to the situation which traumatised them. The stress of re-living the situation over and over again causes a significant impact on how they think and react to everyday situations which other people would not think twice about. These triggers could be from any of the senses: a certain smell or sound, a taste or feeling which reminds them of something from the situation, consciously or unconsciously. Additionally, trauma victims can suffer from severe impairment to the functioning of their brains and as such, their bodies.

Adrenaline produced defends the body when it undergoes a threat. As we know, it is our body's response to our panic; the more adrenaline produced, the more accurate your memory of the experience will be. The more we care about something, the more we emotionally, mentally and physically retain the memory of it.

Trauma can also impair the functioning of the victim's brain significantly. It can affect the immune system and the registering of danger, leaving the body over-sensitive to threat and, in turn, attacking the body's own cells when there are no toxins that would usually be the target. In traumatic experiences as well as in the memory of them, the brain regions vital to translate the incoming stimuli and sensations can be severely impaired or shut down completely. The prefrontal cortex, the thalamus and associated areas, which would take the information coming in and process it into our understanding of the experience and also to be used later as an association for future experiences, can shut down completely. The limbic system, the emotional brain, takes control and changes the balance of emotional stimulation. When entire sections used to process new information coming in are unable to process such stimuli, the individual is left with no explanation for the information. No explanation or story of what the incoming information is can lead to serious mental and emotional issues, and the individual would be unable to understand or deal with what they are experiencing. Appropriate threat responses will be experienced even in non-threatening situations,causing a multitude of debilitating effects on the emotional, mental and physical body.

"The lower brain shuts down completely from being completely overwhelmed by hyper arousal. Dissociation occurs and then hypo arousal occurs (a shut-down of metabolic state).In essence collapse of the right brain. Without metabolic energy, the functions are gone, the affective state that accompanies the collapse of the right brain would be intense hopelessness and helplessness."

Dr Allan Shore www.psychalive.org

Basically a person would be trapped in the inability to help themselves and seek treatment or help from others. It is one of the main components leading to suicide. Many victims lose their entire memory/ knowledge of abuse and suffer strange physical symptoms with no explained physical cause; until triggered memories or flashbacks occur, where suddenly they spiral back into the experience as though it was happening again at the very moment. There is no memory processing in dissociative states. Without the understanding of the trauma and processed memory, they are left in shock and fear and an inability to deal with what is happening to them in the same way as a person with full functioning memory and system would. Dissociation occurs when the individual is unable to process the memories of the trauma. They shut down, in order to forget the trauma. Parts of the brain and function are shut down and impaired, and because of this, the individual is unable to create new emotional comprehension of any new experiences coming in. They lose themselves by shutting down the memories of their trauma. They can feel detached from their own experiences and from their own body. This can be studied more in depth, and this is just a brief explanation with regard to the functioning of the body under stress and in relation to adrenaline.

Another hormone which plays an important role is dopamine. dopamine is said to be received by numerous parts of the brain, including the hippocampus, amygdala, nucleus accumbens, striatum and the prefrontal cortex. The ventral tegmental area of the midbrain passes on the signals, releasing dopamine,a neurotransmitter and hormone that has a significant role in body function, memory, mood, attention, pleasure, motivation and movement. It is a precursor to adrenaline and very high or low levels of it can be linked to numerous mental illnesses and neurological diseases. It is linked to how our habits and pleasures, and certain pleasurable habits, can transform into addictions.

INJURY TO THE BODY

There are a number of causes and types of injuries to the body which can cause deep emotional distress, and which in turn, can change a person's behaviour, thought patterns and personality significantly. Some are obvious and some are not. Injury and illness can change a person not just on a physiological level but also on a mental level. The body's responses and processes have been altered, which causes a change in the way our brain will respond and how it will process our behaviour and reactions to said response; we can also experience a significant emotional change from this.

Because our brain, body and mind are constantly working together in order for us to function healthily, it is important to take care of each of them. It's possible for us to live without a functioning body with the use of machines and technology, and it is possible for us to be physically able but without full use of our brain and the mental capacity to function efficiently; however this is not an ideal state to be in if possible.

EMOTIONAL RESPONSES

The areas involved in emotion are the thalamus, hypothalamus, amygdala and hippocampus, which come together to form the limbic system. Our emotions are responses to the sensory information we receive.

While the hippocampus has direct involvement with our memory, the thalamus processes the senses and then sends on certain selected signals. Most of the motor and sensory signals are relayed through the thalamus. Think of it, for example, as being similar to a train station, with trains (signals) stopping by at the station (thalamus) before passing on to different areas.

Other inputs come in from the prefrontal cortex and reach the amygdala. Both of these regions are involved in the process and response which creates fear and anxiety. Fear can be produced from the cortex without the amygdala. Think back to our previous look into stress and hormones - our body reacts to threatening situations in a number of ways, we feel a change in temperature or even break out into a cold sweat, our hearts start racing, we feel an energy surge, or we feel shaky and dizzy, and blood is diverted from the stomach to the muscles.

What is stress exactly? Is it based on fear? When the body processes these responses, it understands them as fear. It reacts to our stress as a response to fear. Anxiety is theorised as how the brain responds to stress. The cause of stress is ALWAYS your PERCEPTION of the situation, which is determined by your past painful experiences.

Stress can cause significant physiological changes in our bodies through the way we respond to it. It affects us psychologically, which then affects us physiologically and this, in turn, affects us psychologically further, becoming a cycle. It can cause insomnia, changes in our blood pressure, cause and intensify anxiety and lead to depression and other symptoms and problems. These all feed off each other, so the worse you are feeling, the less sleep you are getting, and the more poorly you are feeling physically will intensify your emotions and emotional response to the stressful situation, which in turn leads you to stay up later at night thinking about it, and repeating the same cycle of poor health and response.

In a similar way, pain can cause both physical and emotional responses in our bodies. If we are emotionally distraught and feel intense and painful emotions, our physical pain can be intensified in our experience of it.

Depending on the emotional reaction and affect on our bodies, pain can either be increased or decreased as it is processed by our bodies. The descending analgesic system releases enkephalins and endorphins which reduce pain; but imagine you are being attacked violently; you will have a very extreme or negatively affected emotional experience associated with how you feel pain; you will be upset or distraught and will feel awful – increasing the level of pain which you feel.

Now if you were rescuing someone and were injured in the process, for example; you would be rushing off adrenaline and endorphins, and most likely could be feeling like a hero, most likely you will not even feel the injury or very minimally compared to if you were the victim in the situation. Our bodies and the feeling of pain are deeply affected by our emotions. In the midbrain, descending pathways inhibit pain transmission at the point of entry. The modulation of pain transmission is activated by the central tegmental nucleus and nucleus raphe; which is why no two people will feel the same degree of pain, even if experiencing the same cause of injury. Psychological factors activate the nuclei, and they release their output, and these same psychological factors influence how we feel pain. This is called pain perception.

MEMORY

We have different types of memory, which are then divided into further types.

We have the working memory, which is our short-term recollections - this "works out" what to do with new information coming in -and we have long-term memory, which is then divided into declarative memory; and then there is the episodic memory and semantic memory. Our declarative memory uses conscious recollection of events, situations and facts. Our semantic memory relates to recalling facts such as numbers, words, and concepts, and is essential in our use of language. Our episodic memory is our recollection of everyday events.

We also have sensory memory.

Implicit memory is unconscious and does not need our ability to recall information consciously, for example - breathing and procedural memory, for example - riding a bike. Explicit memory is the opposite, as a conscious recollection of information.

All of these work in the daily function of our lives to allow us the ability to react and respond unconsciously and consciously.

At times we can have memory problems, which can dramatically affect our responses. Let's look at echoic memory. For example, have you ever had a conversation with someone, or at least tried to have a conversation with someone; only to be met with responses such as "huh", "what?", or "excuse me?". Have you ever had to repeat yourself multiple times only for the person to respond as though they had heard you correctly the first time? This is because their mind has not fully processed what you have said before responding. They are still unconsciously processing the information coming in. They have heard the information; however, it is still being processed in order to be understood.

There are also some people who suffer from amnesia, which can greatly affect a person's life. Many illnesses and disorders relating to memory have a significant impact on behaviour.

According to Takashi Kitamuri, and his studies in optogenetics; short-term and long-term memories are put in place at the same time. Because the cortical memory is not immediately accessible, this was only found out when an optogenetic switch in the neuron involved was activated. The cells which are not immediately accessible mature over time and after approximately two weeks, the long-term memory is formed.

Our memory, in general, works to serve us in our day-to-day functioning and enables us to recall previous experiences. However, neural activations in the recollection of a memory require a change in certain connections. So, a memory is not remembered as such, but rather it is recollected and reconstructed. This is why the memories that we think of often, are not always correct, and as they actually happened; they become less accurate each and every time we recollect them.

THE FIVE LEVELS OF CONSCIOUSNESS

- Conscious
- Non-conscious
- Pre-conscious
- Subconscious
- Unconscious

CONSCIOUS

/ˈkɒnʃəs/

adjective

aware of and responding to one's surroundings. having knowledge of something.

- Oxford Languages

Our conscious is our awareness of ourselves and that which surrounds us.

Our non-conscious processes the information which will not go into our long-term memory. We are not consciously aware of it or the body's processes relating to it. It can be automatic.

Our pre-conscious processes the information which we don't need at the present time but may need in the future. It is not a part of our conscious unless triggered by events and many times is surprising to us to realise that we had the information without consciously taking note of it, meaning that emotions or memories can be recalled.

Our subconscious stores information which we can access if needed. It influences many of our behaviours and emotions, even though we may not be fully aware of it.

Our unconscious mind organises, removes and stores information as needed, without our awareness of it doing so.

Our brains try to create context from all the different information coming in from our senses. It relates information to previous experiences and responses; it takes sensory information coming in and tries to make sense of it in order for it to be useful to us. By using introspection, we can look at our thoughts with the use of our consciousness to understand what is happening in our mind and how we are responding from it.

Reticular formation is the "main switch" of our cerebral cortex, and maintains the functioning which creates our consciousness. By keeping our entire cerebral cortex active, we can receive sensory information, which allows us to make voluntary movements and for the sensory information to be registered by the according lobes. Reticular formation is the connection of the intralaminar nuclei of the thalamus to the cerebral cortex. When we are awake, we can make voluntary movements and understand the different sensory stimuli being received by our bodies, such as visual, hearing and touch. When we are asleep, reticular formation is reduced, and we are not conscious of the sensory information being received, nor do we make voluntary movement unless awoken. We are not conscious of what is happening around us.

So, without going too deeply into Neuroanatomy and function for the average reader, how does this affect us? Our brain receives constant information through our senses. We use our senses to feel, touch and see, to taste and smell, and from this we form our thoughts and emotions. If something is not working correctly, this will affect our thinking patterns, our emotional stability and how we function in our daily lives.

Who we are as people is defined by what information is being received and understood by our bodies, and as a result of this, we develop our thoughts and feelings, our personality, and behaviours. Our perceptions are based on our body function, which is then translated back to us through our experience, and we give it meaning or definition. Our environments, and how we perceive them, and our situations and events determine our personality and mindset. It makes us who we are and what we believe in. Our mindsets are formed from perception, which is formed by what our body has experienced, processed and allowed us to understand. An interesting way to look at it is that our thoughts influence and create our emotional responses. Our emotions are reactions to what we have thought. In recognising an emotion being felt, we can identify what the thought which created it is and from there look at how to change our perspective. By changing our perspective of something it will change what we are thinking and therefore, change how we feel about it. Our emotions cause many of the decisions we make in life, which then causes our actions, and from this, we get our outcome. If we are unhappy with an outcome; we need to look back at how it came about, and investigate how and why. Many times this takes us all the way back to how the information was taken in by us in the first place, before our responses and reactions and then feelings and emotions. To fully understand a situation or outcome, we need to understand why and how it came about.

The brain, as such, is vital in our function and survival. Its main function is to regulate behaviour. Its function generates the actions which determine how we live our life, what we are able or unable to do and how we feel. Now the majority of us know this, we learnt the basics at school and are aware that our brain is responsible for much of how and what we do; so why is it that we don't take proper care of it? Why is it that, with the basic understanding that without a healthy functioning brain, we cannot function in a healthy way; we do not do the utmost to ensure we are in the best possible mental state; we do not learn to regulate our emotions and mental state; we do not take time to understand that our mental state does in fact lead to serious body dysfunction and illness.

Many people will exercise, go to the gym, do sport and take care of their bodies through healthy eating habits however their mental state is in disarray. Then there are those with the opposite problem, in which they take little to no care of their bodies and focus purely on their mind. They succumb to illness, are weak and often depressed. How do we find the balance between the two, in order to benefit from a healthy lifestyle?

By understanding how the body, brain and mind are all connected and, in turn, are affecting each other constantly in our daily lives, how do we learn to take better care of ourselves as an entirety?

CHAPTER TWO

COGNITIVE RESPONSES, PROCESSES AND BIAS

There is little difference in people, but that little difference makes a big difference.

That little difference is attitude. The big difference is whether it is positive or negative.

Robert Collier

Your mental/emotional state controls your life. Your mind may not perceive what your eyes see, if you are in the wrong mental state.

Tony Robbins

Cognition

/kɒgˈnɪʃ(ə)n/

noun

the mental action or process of acquiring knowledge and understanding through thought, experience, and the senses.

Metacognition

/ˌmɛtəkɒgˈnɪʃən/

noun

awareness and understanding of one's own thought processes.

Oxford Languages

- metamemory - How aware we are of how we will remember things.
- metacomprehension - Awareness of language comprehension.

Cognitive Biases are attitude- and belief-based, while Cognitive Distortions are thought patterns; they are negative outlooks on reality and cause poor mental health and lack of efficacy. Cognition doesn't rely solely on the objective or the stimuli but rather on the reconstruction in our minds based on the thoughts, feelings and desires from our past experiences.

Cognitive Bias can be divided into four types:

Attentional Bias: refers to when an individual pays more attention to their negative feelings.

Interpretive Bias: refers to how an individual interprets ambiguous information.

Explicit Memory Bias: refers to an individual consciously trying to remember positive or negative memories.

Implicit Memory Bias: refers to the unconscious of an individual.

COGNITIVE BIAS

Biases are subjective perceptions that we have which determine our behaviours towards our environment.

We can have numerous biases toward life, and they affect us in different ways. Some, such as placebo effect, outcome bias, and stereotyping, can cause detrimental problems if not taken into account.

Bias comes in all different sizes, and we need to look at how we perceive a person or situation before allowing our biases to control and limit us in life.

Our actions are all outcomes of cognitive processes which are influenced by our cognitive distortions.

COGNITIVE DISTORTIONS

Often the thoughts we think can be distorted and unhealthy, they can affect how we feel and our mood, they affect our attitude, and they change the way we feel. Feelings change how we see ourselves and the world, and in turn, how we react to our environment. Let's look into some of the distortions that can affect us.

Deletions are when we concentrate purely on part of a situation in order to focus on what we are doing, but they can also be where we focus purely on the negatives of a situation. This can lead us to the perception that the entire situation is bad, instead of considering all aspects of it, sometimes even overlooking important positive features completely. This works hand in hand with the mental filter in which we view a situation. Often, we filter our experiences and magnify the negative from the limiting beliefs of past experiences.

This leads us to believe that future events will be the same. Imagining their disastrous outcomes and creating out-of-proportion magnifications of events can cause us to come up with poor conclusions that are usually out of reason, leading to extreme emotions and reactions which may possibly have been worked out in a simple way without all the excess drama. We cause ourselves more stress and anxiety over nothing.

Polarised thinking can lead us to believe that there is no in-between in a situation. It is either right or wrong. Success or failure. Yes or no. When often, there is a middle ground which may benefit us. Compromise and taking into perspective that there may be an option in-between, which will be a more balanced approach to things.

Generalisation and stereotyping a situation or person can lead to all kinds of limiting situations: poor relationships, lack of understanding and missing out on valuable opportunities because of not interacting with certain people or environments due to our prejudice, stereotypes or general viewpoints from previous experience or limited perception.

Conclusions and expectations can lead us to come up with an outcome before it has even happened. It can lead us to be disappointed, but more than anything, it can cause us to enter into a situation with preconceived bias and limited beliefs of how it should be. It can cause significant problems in our relationships and how we go on to interact with those around us.

Victimisation and personalising every situation by making it about ourselves can cause us to misinterpret situations and often causes further problems in relationship issues by not taking into consideration other viewpoints, validating another person's feelings and situation or by not accepting that it has nothing to do with us on a personal level at all. Playing the victim will limit us in our behaviours and outcomes in life as well as cause relationship issues with those around us due to us constantly feeling personally attacked. It can also lead us to poor attitudes and unhealthy habits of always blaming others, blaming our environment and not taking responsibility for ourselves. The world seems like an unfair place and everyone is out to get us.

Entitlement and playing the martyr can cause significant issues as well; if we feel we are entitled, we will have certain expectations in situations which may never be met, unless we ourselves actually meet them. Martyrs will delude themselves that they need to take on the responsibility of others constantly in order to be worthy or as an excuse for certain behaviour.

Our feelings can be confused with fact, and we can think that certain beliefs are true and that we have to follow them constantly which then justify actions, behaviours and thoughts, whether they are negative or wrong. We use emotional reasoning to decide and make choices in life often without any fact or truth. We minimise events or situations in denial of whether they are really affecting us and need to be examined and possibly reevaluated.

Memory bias can cause us to misinterpret future situations based on our memories of past experiences. It can cause us to stereotype and judge people or events due to belief systems that we have subconsciously stored in our memories as fact, usually stemming from our childhood and our parents or family members beliefs that were taught and handed down to us. We also tend to make decisions based on what those around us do, instead of taking the time to evaluate a situation and decide for ourselves. Often these conclusions are limited and incorrect, yet no one has taken the time to consider and evaluate it them for themselves.

There are many more and equally limiting distortions that affect our lives on a daily basis, yet most of these, if taken into consideration, can be eliminated purely by sitting down and examining why. Why do we feel this way, why do we think this way, why is it true or fact, and is it real or just a feeling?

EMOTIONAL RESPONSES

If we are aware of how we are interpreting information, if we are aware of our perception of a situation; we will be able to change the said perception which then reduces our interpretive bias and will affect all others. If we can change the way we think about things, we can influence our attentional bias or focus on to more positive feelings and thoughts. By doing this, we can reduce anxiety and stress. The cognitive processes are responsible for regulation of our mood, but also affect our moods; by this, we understand that how we are feeling will affect how we think. If we can understand the reasons and processes of how we think and feel, and how we acquire knowledge and information which then creates our thought processes, we can then understand how to change them in order to resolve issues of stress, depression and anxiety. By doing this, we can "input the correct things, in order to output the right things".

Let's look at in more simple terms. Our emotions are reactions to what we feel, and if we recognise what it is that we are feeling, we can then identify the negative thought, we can then change the thought or thought process, and this, in turn, will change the emotion. If you are able to control your thoughts and thought processes you will be able to control your emotions, which will control your mood, your entire mindset and your mental state. Our emotions cause our decisions which lead to how we react and act in our daily lives. These actions produce results in our lives. If we are not happy with the results, we need to look at how they came about. If you are not getting the result you want, it is your responsibility to make the changes necessary in order to get the result you are wanting.

Where do emotions come from? What is the cause, and how can we change them? How do we know where to start?

The most important part of change is how you feel about it. In change, you need to feel good about it, you need to want to change and feel as though you will benefit from it. You must fully believe and understand that your life will improve after changing. If you are feeling anxious or unsure or have negative thoughts and feelings towards change, then most likely, you will not ever take the leap and start working towards it.

One of the major obstacles people come across is fear. Fear of consequences, fear of taking action, as well as fear of embarrassment/failure or of what others will think of them. However, what they fail to realise is, that most people are more interested in their own lives to care, and if they do care and cause any negativity, it's most likely that these are not people you should be surrounding yourself with anyway. It's most likely that you would not want these people around in the future, and it is probably due to many feelings associated with them that has caused the fear in the first place. This will continue in other aspects and areas of your life. The people you should surround yourself with should be those who support you and help you grow as a person, those who have been there as you evolve and appreciate you. Sometimes when going through changes or realising we would like to change certain aspects of our lives, we realise that the people surrounding us are in fact not at all the types of people we would like to be associated with. Without working out your values, wants and needs; you may not even realise this beforehand.

If we have no basis on which to judge our connections and environment, we are merely going through life experiencing it as it happens to us, with no direction or definite opinion of what we want from it. We allow negativity in from others and our environments simply because we have not taken the time to realise that we do not want those aspects around us. We allow negativity to affect us continuously by not taking responsibility for how we deal with our surroundings. No stable person would purposely choose negativity over positivity, so the more you start to think about these questions and about your life, the more you will start to notice the patterns and behaviours associated with them. However this is where it gets more complicated.

Many of us fear cutting others off, putting up boundaries and moving out of or changing our environments. These actions can possibly cause anger from others and possible physical and/or emotional altercations with those around us, who may find it offensive. Moving out of an environment that you have known for most of your life or even just an extended period of time can be a big step. Fear of the unknown can also be frightening without a clear view of where you are going and what you will changing for. Without a clear view and idea in place, change might be altogether too frightening even to attempt. Some people could be acting and thinking out of subjectivity, through their empathy for those who are causing the negativity in their lives, and feeling guilty for wanting change, and as such they may not be looking at the situation logically for what it really is. There could be financial constraints or familial constraints, and this overall can seem daunting and too much to deal with, becoming so overwhelming that change is then avoided, discarded and forgotten about, leaving the person to continue in their current situation without any progress.

CHAPTER THREE

PERCEPTION ~ PERSPECTIVES

Perception

/pəˈsɛpʃ(ə)n/

noun

1. the ability to see, hear, or become aware of something through the senses.
2. the way in which something is regarded, understood, or interpreted.

Perspective

/pəˈspɛktɪv/

noun

a particular attitude towards or way of regarding something; a point of view.

As defined by Oxford Languages

The most important element of good communication is hearing what isn't said.

Peter Druker

IDENTIFYING CAUSES OF LIMITING BELIEFS, CURRENT SITUATIONS AND HOW THESE ARE AFFECTING US

We are not disturbed by the things that happen to us, but rather by the view we take of the things that happen.

Epictetus

Have you ever thought to yourself: "Is what I am thinking the truth of the situation?" or "Is what I believe the true fact?" There are many versions of these two questions with varying situations; however, the principle remains the same - how do we know that what we see, think and believe is in actual fact true?

You will always tell a story from your own preconceived ideas, experiences and expectations. No matter who you are or what you believe in, we all have this same response, whether conscious or unconscious. This is why, often, in order to change a certain outcome, we need to change the way in which we look at things. These presets as it may, can influence our lives a great deal, right down to small decisions and thoughts in our daily lives, without us even realising it, and is how two people looking at the exact same situation can see something completely different to each other. Two people can be in the same position or the same situation and end up with a completely different outcome.

So how do we choose the better outcome? How do we understand that there is always a choice, and that, ultimately, it is our responsibility to make the right choice no matter what the circumstances? That even in traumatic or uncontrollable events, it is our choice and responsibility to choose to react in a way that benefits us and not let the situation or event control us.

Something of great significance to me, for example, is when reading a book inherited from my grandmother on psychological practice and theories; I noticed that she had highlighted completely different sections of text to what had stood out to me as being of importance. This was a woman I hold in very high regard, who was intelligent, wellread, and of outstanding values. I consider myself to take after her in many ways; as I grew up very close to her, we shared similar values, and background, and she taught me many things which I still adhere to today. Yet, we saw completely different insight of items of importance in the same book.

We read the same book, the same words and explanations, and yet we hold completely different sections of text as guidance and to add to our knowledge on certain topics and understanding on certain principles. It was not a personal book or anything that could be read as other than fact.

What does this mean?

Perception, understanding and interpretation are based on our own personal experience and mental state, rather than being based on the truth of the actual fact or the reality of the situation. This is why our beliefs and perceptions of people do not define who they really are as a person, they are not factual and are held differently by each person coming into contact with that same person by using previous experiences to define their current experience, whether consciously or not. This is why two people in the same exact situation can have extremely different emotions, opinions and understandings of the exact same thing.

This is why, it is always important to approach situations and experiences or discussions with an open mind, to stay unbiased and consciously keep our personal experiences, beliefs and opinions clear when analysing, thinking, listening and creating; so as not to be biased by our own limiting belief systems or mental state, that could hinder our full understanding of the entire situation.

When having a discussion with someone, listen to understand and not to respond. Stay quiet to take in all the information. Take note of your mental and emotional state. Then respond with clear and un-obscured understanding.

What does this have to do with behaviour, how we function and how we feel about our lives? What does this have to do with transforming our lives for the better?

Everything.

PERCEPTION

As no one else can know how we perceive, we are the best experts on ourselves.

Carl Rogers

Our perceptions of ourselves have been created over years of life experience, and through this, we adopt coping mechanisms. Sometimes these behaviours can be unhealthy and can often take us completely by surprise;at other times, we are aware of them but aren't sure why we reacted in a certain way. It could even be that we don't want to behave that way and understand that we should not behave in a certain way, yet somehow we find ourselves reacting in a way which is far from how we would really hope to behave.

Often the ideologies that we function from are passed down to us from our upbringing, our parents and family members, our educational experiences, cultural and societal influence. Experiencing unhealthy emotions is a key symptom of poor perception and unhealthy cognitive processes.

When we react and respond from perception, it means that our reaction/response will not likely be directly from what we are looking at but from how we are looking at the situation/event. Our reaction then, may not be an objective one as we will be using our beliefs and pre-existing ideals to understand the situation and in turn react to it. If our perception is based on unhealthy ideals, beliefs and experiences, then it will most likely turn out that we will react in an unhealthy way.

Sometimes we react without responsibility of ourselves; we avoid it with denial, we repress an event, we act out with inappropriate behaviour, we say inappropriate things.

There are many ways in which we deal with situations in an unhealthy manner, including dissociation, displacement, regression, sublimation, projection or rationalizing our behaviour - trying to explain away our unhealthy thoughts and reactions. These all play an important role in how we perceive our life to be and react in situations. All our thoughts and experiences are impressed upon our mind in some form or other, whether subconsciously or not, and this influences our perceptions, whether we are aware of it or not.

Have you ever been in a situation and thought of something regarding it, only to think to yourself, why would I even think that? Sometimes a situation can trigger a deeply buried memory, which causes thoughts that you would not normally associate or want to associate to the particular situation.

PERSPECTIVES

Let's look at an example:

Imagine you are a male/female living in a city where a certain religion is practiced and followed. Your perception of the religion will determine your beliefs of that said religion. (Please note this is NOT a debate on whether the religion or any other religion is true or not true, and nor is this book in any way about religion or whether any religion as a belief is true or not; but in fact in this example, how we perceive and understand it to be from our experience of it. It can be used for any religion or in another context as a general example of perspective).

Now imagine how the sensory information regarding your experience is being taken in: you use your eyes to read about it, you see and experience the practice of the religion in the religious setting/building or your home; you use your ears to listen and learn about it - you hear the sermons and other's viewpoints on the religion and it's practices and principles, you hear the music and songs, and so forth.

Now, the majority of us will have previous experience of religion and our past experiences with it will affect how we are imagining it to be as we read through this example, whether we are trying to be unbiased or not; so here I will give you two different perspectives.

The first perspective is that you have grown up in a positive environment, where said religion has been introduced and enjoyed. It is uplifting and based on positive outlooks and mindsets without, or with minimal judgement and limitations. It is embracing and inclusive.

The second perspective is that you have grown up in a negative environment, where said religion has been enforced through fear and guilt. You were forced to attend and practice, you were punished if you did not act according to the preconceived ideals of the religion, or you were made to feel inferior, or in some cases, abuse was involved. You would have a very different outlook on the same religion. Your perspective would be completely different to that in the first example, wouldn't it? Without giving any proof of the validity of the said religion, it would provide very different sets of beliefs regarding it.

In general, people's beliefs are not based on fact but rather on how they feel about the situation/thing/person or event. Two people exposed to the exact same religion can have very different perspectives. They can read the same text, hear the same sermon and songs, and be sitting next to each other in the same religious setting; however they can have very different feelings on what they are experiencing. There are many different perspectives of the same thing, and we will never know or understand all of them, as they are based on personal experience; but we can understand that by looking at our perspectives and how we deal with them, can affect how we respond and react to others and how our personalities and beliefs are formed.

Beliefs then determine how we feel and behave.

So, using the same example, someone with the belief that they are supported and in a positive environment is more likely to take positive actions and have positive feelings, whereas the opposite can be said of the person experiencing negative situations or environments. Our behaviours are linked directly to how we feel and how we perceive a situation to be, without any regard for the actual truth of it. It doesn't matter whether we are right or wrong, however it is important with how we see, understand and then act according to our perceptions. If we believe we are right, but have a negative perception and then act out in a negative manner; this will cause an even more negative environment. By us believing that we are correct in having this belief without taking into consideration other perspectives or facts, we are then enforcing our limiting, biased beliefs on those around us. It becomes a cycle. This is one of the leading causes of many of our issues in life. It is not the problem itself but our perception and, in turn, behaviour and reactions towards it. If we are not open to new perspectives and understanding, we will remain in the negative cycle, leading us into depression and anxiety.

WHAT ARE OUR PERCEPTIONS AND HOW DO THEY COME ABOUT?

Perceptions are based on personal experience however many are influenced heavily by certain things such as our culture, our educational experience, our peers and social group, our family background and our parents perceptions which we have grown up to incorporate into our own or have discarded and based our perceptions on the complete opposite of what our parents demonstrated to us, our social status and our economic situation or class. We begin our lives, learning everything from our parents and families and home environment, it influences everything that we believe or don't believe in and how we see the world. It is where, the start of our personalities and our interests are formed; and is also where we start to look at ourselves and who we are as individuals, how we expect to be treated by others and how we believe we should behave, feel, think and learn..

It forms the basis of who we are. We then move onto school, and slowly add in more experiences where we can judge, alter and further define ourselves and how we see the world around us. This continues throughout our lives as we experience new environments, people and situations. Every single thing that we are exposed to or experience will have some sort of impact on our lives, whether it is small or significantly impactful.

PERCEPTION INFLUENCING BEHAVIOUR

Carl Rogers created a theory of perception and self with different propositions in order to evaluate how we understand the world around us and our lives. We can look at how we can be influenced in life based on theories such as this.

- Is the only perspective you can appreciate your own? Are you able to listen, accept and understand other perspectives?

- Is your perspective of reality truly what is happening around you? Are there opposing facts and beliefs, and if so, what are they and why? Are you aware of your surroundings in their entirety?

- Are you dealing with the effects of a situation or the situation itself? Is there avoidance taking place or denial of the cause of a situation?

- Are you defining yourself by your ideals? Or defining your identity by what and how you live?

- Are we influenced by those around us? Beliefs handed to us by our parents and those we grew up with? Are we influenced by our culture and society, or are we able to come to our own conclusions?

- Is our intention that of good value?

- Have you taken the time to understand the situation or other person completely, why they believe what they do, or what causes their behaviours and reactions; in order to respond effectively?

- Are you able to understand why you are driven to do the things you do in life? Are you aware of what is motivating and influencing your choices and goals?

- Are your emotions controlling your behaviours?
- Are your values at the core of what you do virtuous, and are you behaving in a way that is of worth?
- Are you dismissing the opinions and experiences of others because you disagree with them? Or are you able to relate to alternative and contrasting viewpoints?
- Are you comparing yourself to others? Are you confident in yourself and your beliefs and understanding?
- Are you able to change and make important changes when necessary?
- Do you accept responsibility for yourself at all times?
- Do you perceive others as a threat? Are you able to function alongside others in a productive manner?
- Do your actions, beliefs and thoughts stem from positive intentions?

PERCEPTUAL REPOSITIONING

Perceptual positions or repositioning refers to the technique of looking at a situation/event from a different perspective. Possibly this is something you have done before. Have you ever looked at someone as if you were them? Have you ever looked at a situation as though you were not actually a part of it? The process enables a person to experience a situation through three different sensory perspectives: ourselves, another person and an objective, unbiased person who is not a part of the situation or event.

Perceptual repositioning is a valuable tool to help us understand a situation better in order to see why someone may have treated us or interacted with us in a way with which we disagreed, it can help us to look at something from a different view in order to come up with a different conclusion and outcome (this can help significantly with nervousness and anxiety as well as in situations of trauma) and it can help us to evaluate our decisions and choices by taking into consideration every angle of the situation.

Often, unless we step back and look at how we are reacting or behaving, we may not take it into consideration whatsoever. No second thought or understanding that the way in which we are reacting and thinking may be contributing to or determining the outcomes in our lives. Looking at the situation from different angles or opposite viewpoints allows us to examine our behaviours and thoughts by taking the time to really consider why and how we are reacting and allowing a situation to control our emotions and how we can possibly change this.

Let's look at how to use this technique in everyday life:

Start by thinking of an event or situation that has kept you up at night; wracking your brain, disturbing your thoughts and upsetting you repeatedly each and every time it pops into your mind. If it is easier, you can write down everything as you go along with the process. Sometimes getting it down on paper can help you to go back and reflect and also, by reading it back to yourself, you will better understand the opposing viewpoints.

Now think of this situation and how it makes you feel. Imagine you are in the situation and think about how you are interacting with the person or in the event that took place; picture the other person/object and how they were behaving. Imagine everything that happened or was said and how you felt.

Now, imagine you are the other person or the opposition of your viewpoint (to avoid confusion I will still refer to you as yourself). Imagine why they approached you regarding this situation, or if you had approached them, how they felt as you approached them. Imagine that someone had approached you in that manner. What are the reasons behind their original behaviour which caused the situation in the first place? How are they feeling because of it? And now, how are they feeling about the entire situation and the result of it? How is or would this affect their future or life? Are their reasons behind it related to how they feel would best protect their interests, themselves, family, job etc; are their reasons related to how you feel and are they intentionally trying to hurt you or cause distress in your life? Are they doing what's best for them? Are they taking you into consideration? Imagine and think of everything you are able to about their side of the situation.

Now, imagine yourself as someone who was not involved, with no emotional investment in the situation and no bias toward either side of the situation. How would you feel about it? How would you view the situation and feel would be the correct way to go about things? Imagine and think of everything you are able to as an outsider in the situation.

By doing this, you can now go back to your viewpoint on the situation. Do you still feel the same way about what happened? Do you still feel your perception of the situation is correct or the only viewpoint? Does the entire situation seem more reasonable or logical? Do you feel more of an understanding as to why you received this particular treatment from the opposing side? Does this change the outcome? Does this change your perspective and perception of the situation and similar situations like it?

Usually, this technique gives us significant insight and can really help with dealing with situations and problems that arise in our lives. Being able to approach life with an open mind and not take our perception of events as fact; allows us to deal more effectively with those around us, to come to better conclusions and outcomes and to feel better about our interactions with those surrounding us and our environment.

People, in general, have a tendency to look for the negative rather than the positive in a situation or experience. Often they will react out of fear or may not act at all in social settings, rather than be the person to act out of confidence who takes an opinion or stance in front of their peers. Many will react, but few will act of their own accord. Many more will react when they feel there is no regulation of responsibility over their behaviours and responses. It is cowardly in its avoidance and lack of culpability of one's own self.

Think through how you have reacted in the past in different situations and experiences, and see if you can take a different perspective and ask how this affects your perception toward it. You never know; you may just stumble upon something which will change the way you view things or may even resolve an issue you have been suffering from for a very long time.

CHAPTER FOUR

THINKING PATTERNS, BEHAVIOURS AND BELIEFS

Opinion lives between truth and complete ignorance
- Plato

Are our opinions limiting us in our daily lives, are they causing an unnecessary negative impact on our lives and future, are they based on sound reasoning or from fear? Unproductive, unhelpful and negative thinking patterns cause us to have, and react in, unproductive and negative behaviours and feel undesirable emotions. If we are emotional and feeling negative emotions, we will most likely react to others and events out of subjectivity rather than looking at a situation objectively with sound reason and insightful wisdom. We will possibly miss the truth of the situation for not comprehending the entirety of it or for focusing solely on our feelings about the situation. How we respond and react determines others attitudes towards us. How we treat others determines others treatment of us. How we behave determines the behaviour of those around us.

What we focus on in life influences us and how we feel. What we focus on the most, we usually end up getting... whether it is good or bad, whether it is what we want or what we don't want. Have you heard the saying: whether you think you can or you can't, either way you are right by Henry Ford? Believing in what you are capable of or what you are not capable of has a significant impact on whether we achieve our dreams and goals. If you have a strong belief in yourself and a strong sense of self, confidence and self-esteem, you are more likely to be able to accomplish what you put your mind to. the same thing applies if you do not believe in yourself and believe you are incapable - you will most likely get nowhere and even more so, achieve nothing. If you don't believe that you can, nine times out of ten, you won't even try. This relates to what is called the Pygmalion Effect or self-fulfilling prophecy.

Beliefs are not factual. They are the ideas we have learned and then validated through the experiences in our life. They are nothing more than an idea or opinion, yet many of us have beliefs and ideals that limit us in many ways, a set of rules that we live by, what we should or shouldn't do and what we can and can't do. They determine our actions toward both ourselves and to those around us.

LIMITING BELIEFS

What you have not been exposed to or have not experienced; cannot be understood nor can it be overcome. Individuals will always expect for the future, that which they have experienced previously, or that which they have been exposed to previously.

How an individual perceives themselves determines how they interact with their environment and whether this interaction is beneficial or not. Our beliefs of ourselves start the cycle which determines the outcome of any interaction we are part of; they influence our actions and behaviours towards others which, in turn, impact the other person's beliefs of us and thus their behaviour towards us in return.

Let's look at a few limiting beliefs. These are generally how a person perceives themselves to be. They can believe that they are too old or too young; they cannot start/change/do something because they are not the right or appropriate age to do so. They may feel that they cannot compete with others of a different age group or that they are physically unable to because of their age, without having substantial proof or facts to confirm this. They can believe they are not intelligent enough, or they are too stupid or do not have the right education, or not enough knowledge or skill, without having attempted to gain any further insight or knowledge or without verifying that they do not in fact, have the right skills and enough intellect and knowledge.

It could be that they feel guilt or that they are not deserving enough to have more. They might believe that they are not good enough, or as good as someone else, or that they have not done enough yet or have not come from a background or culture where what they want is feasible or popular, and so they never take a chance or put in any effort or try. They could be scared or embarrassed by what others will think or say about them, or they could believe that they could not afford to or that they should put other people's priorities before their own at all times. These are among many, many other beliefs that keep us stuck in the same situation without ever attempting to achieve more.

LIMITING BEHAVIOURS

Why is it that in certain social settings, we display different behaviours? In some, we may be strong and loud and impressive, while in others, we may be shy or quiet and victims of circumstance. Our environment dictates our behaviour. What we know we can get away with influences how we associate with different people. What we believe will benefit us most will determine our behaviours. Are they really and truly beneficial behaviours, or do they just prompt instant gratification? Do they help us show who we truly are, or will our behaviours promote and enable monetary gain, sympathy, power, envy and so on?

How would changing these behaviours look? Would we be judged if we changed our behaviours according to people's predetermined beliefs of who we are as a person? By challenging the norm, would that mean we would lose the benefits of instant gratification or would it generate the reward of real respect and beneficial and/or mutually beneficial relationships and situations where we would progress in life? What can be said about us as people and as a society where we allow our environment to dictate our behaviour and our lives to the point where we "change as people" in order to fit in? Most people do this so often that they do not realise it any longer; it has become part of their unconscious way of life.

Examples: we see a parent and instantly become a baby - needing to be taken care of, dependent and incapable. We see a friend and instantly become a victim - sharing all the things that have gone wrong in our lives since we last visited/ saw them. We see our colleagues and instantly become powerful, strong individuals who are competing for success; or in other cases, become meek and fearful, unable to share opinions because they intimidate us or are more successful than us. We see an acquaintance who we don't really like or want to impress or want to instigate envy within them over how "well we are doing in life" and create a false pretence of superiority.

We create these different "personas" constantly, possibly more than one in particular situations with the same people - all in the hopes of getting something out of it. It could be a physical reward such as money - by playing the dependent, our parents might give us money, the bank might give us a loan, our work may give us a raise and so on. By playing the victim, our friend will feel sorry for us, and we will receive attention; by playing the powerhouse we will receive admiration and respect; by playing the success story, we will revel in the envy of others.

But are these really worth it? By being dependent, we do not learn responsibility and when that emotional or financial crutch is no longer available, how will we survive without transferring our dependency onto others? Does sharing all our negative emotions with our friends not overburden them and cause them to feel emotionally drained every time they see us? Does creating this powerful persona really mean that people respect and admire you: or are they scared, or really not very impressed, or just dealing with you to get about their day? Is the respect real, and are you deserving of such respect by having earned it through your efforts? Or are you domineering and abusive in forcing your opinion onto others? Are people truly envious of you, and what is this worth? Wouldn't it be more rewarding to have people like and care for you instead? Wouldn't this lead to people wanting to work or be friends or create opportunities with you in the future and therefore leading to successful respect of you?

How are you consciously or unconsciously behaving in your life towards those around you and in certain situations? Do you realise when you would benefit, and is it for instant gratification, or is it for respectful and genuine benefit? Are you unconsciously playing out a role that gives others a false sense of who you are? And if you are playing a persona in a certain situation, what does this say about your genuineness?

Many times people do not realise this or do not know who they are as a person in order to behave in an appropriate way, demonstrating their true selves. It can cause an individual to end up in all kinds of situations and relationships where when they don't work out or work in their favour, they don't understand why. They question the other person's intentions or judgement, or the situation as a conspiracy against them, without realising their behaviours influenced the entire process.

Without real reason or a substantial need for these behaviours, such as a traumatic instance or grief where we need to speak to someone or be consoled, financial assistance due to an event or situation, or other such instances. Are our reasonings behind our behaviours substantiated by real and significant factors or are they purely for our own satisfaction?

Instant gratification is never the answer; it starts a vicious cycle, chasing short-term pleasures without a long-term goal or achievement in sight. Once the pleasure wears off, we begin the cycle again. This instant self-esteem booster has no foundation to build from in order for us to become the person we truly want to be, and most times, we end up being quite the opposite. For instance the person trying to show off their power, can come across as desperate in trying to grab the attention and admiration of everyone and anyone while never gaining any real respect. Their behaviours will not align with who they are trying to emulate, and they will not achieve their goal of being a revered person of status.

An individual will only change how they feel by the regulation of how they think, behave and what they believe to be true. The attitude, approach and assumptions made by an individual should be positive in order to influence a positive outcome from their environment and from those surrounding them.

If an individual is capable of learning an unhealthy behaviour, they are also capable of "unlearning" it. It is impossible to control the thoughts which enter our minds; however, we can control how we choose to let them affect us. We all have the ability to change our thoughts and our ideas and how we perceive that which we experience; we just need to learn how to do it in a healthy way.

CHAPTER FIVE

DEALING WITH DEPRESSIVE MENTAL STATES AND LABELS THAT DISRUPT OUR DAILY LIVES

Basically all patients come to psychiatrists with one "common" problem; the sense of helplessness, the fear and inner conviction of being unable to "cope", and to "change things". The failure to accept responsibility for their problems and their lives.

Dr Hilde Bruch

What you feel and how you act does not define who you are as a person. Certain actions or feelings that oscillate and are not continued for extended periods, which are caused by or are responses to specific events, experiences or situations, are not defining states of identity.

For example, an individual who is feeling depressed because they are lonely due to not socialising; is not a depressively disordered individual. If they were to socialise or make friends and change their situation, they would no longer be depressed, therefore, it is not a defining characteristic of their identity but rather a feeling they are experiencing due to a situation. Change the situation - change the feeling.

Often, by giving certain labels, we start to define ourselves by that, and that alone. These include our religious beliefs, sexual preferences, job titles, feelings, illnesses, hobbies, marital status and family status, among many others. This is an extremely limiting response to how we perceive ourselves; and can cause us to behave in certain ways in which we are not benefiting ourselves or those around us. It can stop us from attempting anything else we wish to achieve, and it can make us feel stuck in life. Many times we can end up feeling depressed, and we will act a certain way, think a certain way and treat others a certain way. In turn, others will return said treatment in a less than favourable way, and this turns into a way of life. We start to believe that this is just the way life is or should be, and we compromise who we could be for how we feel in the moment. We will be more likely to miss opportunities due to being too focused on how terrible we feel or how bad a situation is, or how we think it should be. From this, others may not even want to share opportunities with us due to our miserable and unproductive state. We can seem uninterested, unreliable or unapproachable.

This is not to be confused with an individual going through a serious traumatic, depressive or other clinically diagnosed disorder or experience; but applies to individuals who superficially use emotions as a crutch or excuse of habit. We have all heard someone say, "I am so depressed..." or "I am so traumatised"...; without there being a significant reason or truly depressive or traumatic experience. Labels are thrown around colloquially with a type of "victim mindset" behind them. This can be harmful for numerous reasons; we no longer take responsibility for ourselves, we start losing our actual self-esteem and become the victim in every situation, we use transference only to find that we are in a state of dependency. We adopt the mindset that we are incapable—

creating unnecessary fear in order to avoid taking the responsibility for our own lives and limiting ourselves from achieving our goals and living the lives we truly wish to, which usually leads to the blame being placed on others as doing otherwise would mean taking further responsibility for our inaction as well. No one wants to be depressed, but many times an individual becomes so comfortable in their ways; that change seems like all too much to undertake, no matter what the benefits could be or the rewards of achieving it. Without the desire to change, without wanting to change more than staying in a state of dependency, an individual will stay in their depressive or limiting state and never implement any change or achieve personal growth. They may see this state as all they will ever be and no way out of it, without ever realising that it boils down to choice.

The choice to make substantial changes in everyday life, which lead to larger goals in the future; and by making better choices, living a better life

The first choice we can make right now is whether we are a victim or the victor.

Think of a traumatic event or experience, something significant that happened to you in the past. Think back to being right there in the moment, what was running through your mind at the time?

Was it: "I am a victim right now"?

Or was it: "I need to survive this"?

The majority of people will describe what they remember as saying to themselves that they needed to survive or get through the situation, to get away, to make it through what they were going through. I have yet to meet someone who has said they thought they were a victim in the midst of the event taking place, although I am sure it is possible. Our instinct is 99% of the time to protect ourselves, to get us to a place of safety and to get through a situation where we are in perceived danger. It is a natural response.

So look at where you are now. You have survived the event, yes you may have some scars to show from it, whether they are physical or emotional but you have in fact survived. If you hadn't survived, you would not be reading this book at this very moment. So my question then is this: why are you taking the victim stance if, in fact, you are a victor? You are a survivor. You survived the situation; you made it through, and you got out of the situation. You were victorious.

Without taking away from the severity of the situation for what it was; is the fear of the situation still holding you captive in an experience to which in fact, you are no longer in? Are you fearful that it will happen again? Are you living as though you are in the situation currently, constantly?

Or are you able to see that in fact, you are a success.

Let's look at this in a slightly different way, labels can cause other limits in our lives where we define ourselves as sick, and unable to do certain things because we are consumed by how we have become defined.

Example:

You feel terrible, you have physical symptoms and you go to a doctor. They tell you are depressed. They prescribe medicine.

The medicine is designed to treat the symptoms and not the problem. No medicine is ever going to be able to fix the problem or give a solution to it; and no matter how long you take the medicine, it will not make the problem go away. It will only treat the physical symptoms of it. Now, this can make it easier to deal with the problem, but no one wants to feel awful forever. We don't want to have to take medicine for the rest of our lives and we don't want to be taking medicine at all if it is not necessary. A general doctor will not be looking for the solution to your depression for you, as they are not trained to do so; they can only offer you relief of the symptoms, and many times an individual is given a quick diagnosis without a proper examination and prescribed medication without any form of examination or help in resolving the issue. This is not to say that medication is bad or that mental disorders and illnesses are not real or don't need medicine at all; however, the most appropriate thing to do is to see a mental health professional, to be examined properly and treated with regard to the entire problem, it's cause and not only based on its symptoms. The appropriate methods of examination and investigation can then be done about why you have this issue in the first place and if there are ways in which to deal with it and either resolve it or if it is necessary, to take medication to help cope with it.

Let me share a further example: When I was younger, I was quite ill. I went to numerous doctors and hospitals for examinations and testing without any resolution to the problem. Doctors misdiagnosed my illness in numerous ways; they ignored my asthma and respiratory problems due to the pneumonia I had in childhood, without fully testing if these were linked and I was diagnosed for multiple illness including cancer, lung disease, depression - the list goes on and on.... There was no substantial basis for each different diagnosis.

They were all completely different diagnoses and far removed from each other as well as from my symptoms. One doctor diagnosed me with depression without even doing any examination whatsoever. I was not depressed whatsoever. I explained to the doctor that I had symptoms related to my asthma and had not been suffering from them for long; it did not change his diagnosis. Now, knowing myself, I knew I was not depressed and that there was some sort of environmental influence on my health or some type of infection. I kept going to different doctors, trying to find out the cause of my illness. Nothing was found whatsoever. I was given all types of medications for the physical symptoms (not depression), and at one stage, I was taking so many different tablets that I was feeling even worse. The medications had such a terrible effect on me and were physically compromising my health. I knew that they were not in anyway helping my situation. I had machines to help me breath and pumps and nebulisers. Would all this have been necessary if we had found the cause?

Eventually, I found the cause myself. It happened through deciding I needed a change of scenery and to redecorate my bedroom. Something like this can help to feel fresh and initiate a new start in life, which I really needed at the time to distract myself from feeling sick. By moving furniture around, we found that the newly renovated bathroom attached to my bedroom had been leaking from under the shower. The wall was covered in damp. This damp had caused an allergy which had caused my respiratory problems and illness. I had never been given any testing related to allergies and I had not ever thought to check for damp in my house. By finding the solution to the issue, fixing it, and discarding the useless medications, my illness was gone. I was feeling 100% once more. There had never been any need for some of the medications I had been prescribed and I had been diagnosed with all kinds of things; some of which can be terrifying to hear, such as cancer, without any proof of having them I had been prescribed medication that I did not need which led me to feel worse and the doctors I had seen had not tried to find the cause in anyway.

This is the problem with many situations; we are quick to assign a label or disease or disorder and to medicate the symptoms, when sometimes all we really need to do is to find the cause behind it in order to solve it. Sometimes medications are unnecessary and it is important to know when they are and when not.

Often in a situation we can feel helpless; we will not know how to deal with something and may not be able to see an end to it. We rely on others to take responsibility for our lives with the hope that they will "fix" us, and in turn, we get nowhere and are sometimes even worse off than when we started. We need to treat the problem and not the symptoms to find a solution. Work out the issue; work out how to change the reason for the issue, and often the issue will disappear. I am not, however, discrediting medical treatment when necessary, many times physical symptoms do need to be treated along with finding a solution; yet many times, our physical symptoms can cause us to be diagnosed with diseases, disorders and the likes of depression when really we just have an unresolved issue that is simply causing these effects. Are we really depressed? Or are we just feeling miserable and awful because we are ill, and if we start to feel better, will these feelings change, or would treating our feelings with medications actually make us feel worse because we are treating an illness which we do not have?

Labels come in many different kinds and have all kinds of negative associations attached to them. When defining an individual by their interests, preferences or status, we then limit them to that and that alone. We are all so much more than just what we do or what we like; we have so much to offer and so much that we are capable of; yet we make assumptions about ourselves and others based off of labels constantly, which box us into what usually has no benefit for anyone involved.

CHAPTER SIX

DEVELOPING A HEALTHY MINDSET

Until you make the unconscious, conscious, it will direct your lives and you will call it fate.

Carl Jung

Self-evaluation is fundamental in order to progress. Understanding oneself and the reasoning behind our thoughts, behaviours and beliefs is the answer to learning to control them.

The best way to look at a situation from a healthy point of view is to question how you feel and think:

Are you being selective in what you hear or your attitude?

Are you making assumptions?

Why are you behaving or thinking in this way? Is the reason based on fact and truth? Is it based on emotion, and are those emotions positive or negative?

Learning to recognise and identify symptoms, unhealthy patterns, beliefs, thoughts or unhealthy habits can help to resolve issues before they escalate into larger and more damaging results. If you are able to notice poor sleep patterns, agitation or worries about a certain situation beforehand or if they can be identified as they occur, then they will not develop into insomnia, or anxiety or depression or into other unhealthy behaviours and side effects. Resolving issues as they occur can make an enormous change in how we relate to life; it eradicates the hours of turmoil stressing over having to still deal with something, how we will deal with it and if we can or can't deal with it. We, therefore, do not doubt our capabilities or mental state, and this in turn does not affect our physical state. The feelings of worry and anxiety about a situation before it has happened will be eliminated by dealing with it as soon as possible, if not at the moment it is occurring. And if we can understand why the situation is happening, we can prevent it from occurring again in the future. Healthy lifestyles are not just about the food we eat and the exercise we do. There is so much more to it; and the most important part being our minds. Our minds influence everything in our life, so to create a healthy life and maintain it; we need to take proper care of how we use our minds.

Let's start with the basics of understanding and noticing that which surrounds us.

Are you responding to the actual experience? Or how you feel about the experience? We will always be exposed to stress, to negativity and to unwanted situations in life. However, it is how we assess the situation and respond which determines the outcome. Changing our perspective can allow us to deal with future events in a more productive and positive way. It does not take away the significance of the event or minimise the feelings we may feel, but it will change how we allow it to affect us and our lives thereafter. This changes how it affects our personal lives or work lives and social lives, and our relationships and friendships and our environment, allowing us to maintain our integrity and inner peace regardless of the circumstances

Are you listening to what is being said to you, or are you listening to what you believe a person is saying in order to respond to them? Listening can be one of the most helpful and important tools in life. Often when engaging, we do not actually listen in full to what a person is saying, which can cause all kinds of miscommunication, and frustration, leading to further issues, or it could mean that we misinterpret a situation completely. Listening to understand a person is one of the most valuable abilities to have; not only can it change how we interact with others, but it can lead to opportunities, better relationships and clearer perspectives.

Are you judgemental about or biased against an individual or group? This can lead to all kinds of serious issues. Learning to keep an open mind in all situations can be beneficial in understanding or learning much from what we may never be exposed to by not taking the time to understand that which is different to our own selves.

Judgment can cause many problems in our lives, both with strangers and those we know; by making someone feel uncomfortable it can lead to arguments and even escalate into larger issues. Taking the time to understand can change your interactions with others in many different settings and can lead to opportunities over a wide range of areas.

Do you have preconceived expectations or beliefs of how things should be? This can cause huge disappointment repeatedly, it can cause friction in our relationships, and it can cause us to feel unheard or unappreciated if we do not approach this correctly. It is good to have an idea of what we would like or how we would want something to be. However, having unrealistic expectations or the assumption that everyone should accept and live up to our expectations is one of the main issues in many a relationship (romantic or not). Instead of creating unrealistic standards which have to be met with rules and obligations, it is better to have an open mind while creating a clear and understanding dialogue between those involved and what is needed and necessary, what is wanted and what is possible. Communication is very important so as not to fall into the mistake of assuming that everyone will automatically meet your expectations.

Are you able to recognise your emotional state in different situations and how you may be reacting in different ways when experiencing certain emotions?

By identifying your emotions, you will be more likely to control them. Taking the time to think before reacting can dramatically help a situation, especially when anger, stress or fear is involved.

What is the evidence for the thought or feeling you are currently experiencing? Is the thought or feeling based on fact or is it one in which you are emotional and reacting out of said emotion?

Could it be that you are making an assumption without understanding the entire situation?

Can this situation be interpreted differently? How can it be interpreted differently? Who would interpret it differently, and why would they have a different opinion than you? Is there a balance between these two opinions?

Is this a regular habit?

Is this thought based on fear? What is the reason for your fear? Why is this fear influencing your thoughts on the situation? Is it reasonable? Is this fear a form of avoidance?

There are many different questions that could be asked depending on the exact situation; however the most important thing is to take the time to think and ask why.

Think and ask why before reacting. Think and ask why

when in self-doubt or in fear, misery, uncertainty and anger. In any situation, taking the time to question what you are thinking and why you are thinking it; is the best way to understand how to move forward.

An individual in a stable mindset is aware of their thoughts and emotions, the emotions of others and how their behaviour can and will affect those surrounding them. They are able to control themselves, and exhibit virtuous characteristics. They are wise, of an open mind, courageous, socially intelligent, modest yet confident in their ability, forgiving, gracious and most importantly, practice self-regulation, among others.

Strength of mind can have a significant effect on our lives, yet so many of us fall short for not being exposed to the understanding and knowledge of being able to learn how to achieve it. Many individuals grow up in environments where this is never taught or demonstrated Often throughout life, we are steered to more negative pathways to what would in fact be wise for our psychological well-being and life. While it is not always available to us in early life, we can learn from our experiences in order to get to the point where we take responsibility for our lives in order to improve and succeed.

CHAPTER SEVEN

GOALS AND RESPONSIBILITY OF OUR LIVES

ATTENTION

"Taking possession of the mind, in clear and vivid form, of one out of what seems several simultaneously possible objects or trains of thought. Focalisation, concentration of consciousness are of its essence. It implies a withdrawal from some things in order to deal effectively with others."

- William James

Working out our goals is of great importance in life. Without knowing what we want out of life, how will we ever obtain the life we want?

Is it that where focus goes, action grows? We have all heard and seen trends going around the past few years of manifesting our greatest desires or affirming what you want, and you shall have what you desire.

The law of attraction. Let's take a quick look into this: Does manifestation really exist, or are we creating our desires and goals through increased attention placed on certain aspects of our lives? Is our action or inaction creating these manifestations? We have all heard the expression "Where energy goes, energy flows", but are people misinterpreting this into solely believing into existence the achievement of their desires, goals and dreams? In repeating affirmations mindlessly and listening to sounds which create attraction, to asking a higher power; and not actually taking any action towards achieving or obtaining what they want, by believing it will be automatically handed to them from these beliefs. With manifestation and the law of attraction becoming a trend worldwide, there have been numerous responses to whether this really works or not, with many stating that they lost everything while believing they could manifest what they wanted by repeating affirmations and merely stating to the universe what they wanted.

Why did it not work?

Then there are others who say that they were cured of their cancer or received large amounts of money or promotions. Are people taking quotes, research and facts regarding science and psychology and simplifying them into a misunderstood hypothesis? Many of the quotes shared and information used to prove manifestation and mindsets are, in fact, about achieving goals and putting in the effort. However, this is often surpassed and shared as manifest this or manifest that, by leaving out a substantial part of the information or by pure misinterpretation. Why are some people living the lives of their dreams, and others are left looking as if they have lost their minds; while all claim to follow the same techniques.

The answer is action and mindset. Those who worked out their desires, needs and wants took action towards them. They "manifested" them once they outlined what it was they wanted, then looked at how to obtain them and then slowly but surely worked towards getting to their goal. They made positive changes in their lives with or without realising it, and created a positive mindset which allowed them to see the opportunities surrounding them, which they could then use to their benefit. Talking about something is not the same as doing something about it.

In conditions where we are at risk or not in the right mindset, we are loss averse. We are too scared to take the risk and prefer to make decisions based on what we feel is a "safe bet", even if, statistically, we would come out better by taking the actual risk. When we are in a negative or limited mindset, we do not notice opportunities or make necessary changes and take actions that would benefit us. The more positive you feel about a situation, the more likely you are to benefit from it because you are more likely to put yourself "out there", to engage with others and your environment and to initiate changes. In order to "manifest" what you want, you need to put in the effort to achieve and receive them. You cannot just sit around affirming to yourself without putting it into action. Nothing will happen, which is when you start to question why and what is it that you are doing wrong, and why it isn't working. The uneducated person will take this as being incapable and a failure. Without realising that it is really about working out your goals, what it is you want out of life, and then working towards achieving them. Yes, affirmations can be effective in boosting your self-esteem and eliminating the fear of failure; however, it is the actions we take towards our goals which determine whether we achieve them or not. This applies to every single area of our lives.

Have you ever noticed that when you focus on something, everything else seems to gravitate towards it or suddenly seems to be about it, or you notice it more often in your surroundings? Where when you think of something, suddenly all you see are those things around you in your day-to-day life? Think of a car that you like or that someone has mentioned to you, for example, suddenly everywhere you go, you will start to notice those cars. Our subconscious has always seen these cars, yet somehow, our mind has focused on other "more important things" and wiped them from our vision as if they were never there; yet they were always there. Now when we have that specific car in our conscious mind, we start to see them everywhere as if they are the most popular cars ever. We start noticing them because our mind has been triggered into showing us what we want to see. They have always been there, but were just not in the forefront of our attention.

Similarly, this is how creating our goals works. When your focus and attention go to something, you notice more and more things that can help you in achieving or obtaining what you want, you start to have more ideas on the topic, which can lead to progress, and you notice people and opportunities that could benefit you; thus leading you to success. If you did not work out your goal and had no idea what it was, would you notice something relating to it? Unlikely. If you had a goal but paid no attention to anything related to it or put in any effort regarding it, would you notice anything that could be used as an opportunity? Just as unlikely as not even working it out.

Similarly, when you are nice to someone, they will be more likely to be nice to you, to help you, or to go out of their way for you, whether it is now or at a later stage - creating a beneficial connection based on mutual effort. When you are angry or rude or distasteful, people won't want anything to do with you, and they will most likely avoid you or do anything possible not to have to help you further than necessary; thus, you will lose or miss a possible connection that could help you get one step closer to success.

Our sense of self is a result of our interaction with others and society and our feelings from these interactions.

So are these principles really manifestations or are they simply just goal attainment? The chain effect of creating a goal and taking one simple action, thought or reaction can create a multitude of possibilities which lead us down our different life paths.

We often hear coaches and motivational speakers saying you can do it! Just follow this 12-week programme, or just do these simple steps, and you will have success; you will be the person you want to be, and you will have everything you've ever wanted! Well, why do the majority of people not have this? They hype you up into excitement, and then a few days later you realise you have achieved nothing or have had no progress. Why are people still in bookstores buying the latest self-help book, or at the next motivational speaker's event? Why are they in therapy or coaching? If these simple steps work, then why doesn't every single person who followed them have their desired outcomes?

The answer is simple and has nothing to do with the efficacy in general of the books and speakers or programmes. Most of these programmes and advice are excellent and do work, but you need to put in the work. You need to make the effort. It is up to you to get what you want. No matter who or what you listen to, read or with whom you surround yourself; nothing will start happening until you consciously start making it happen. You need to take responsibility for yourself and your life.

Once you have worked out what it is you want, need or desire, you will have a clear outline of what you would like your life to be like. It gives us our basic idea to start from and from which we can figure out how to get what we want. Without defining what you want and how you want it in detail, how will you know what to do in order to obtain it?

There are numerous ways in which to outline your goals, however, here are a few examples:

Write out a list starting with the most important goals (no matter how large or outlandish), then keep going. You will usually find that once you get going, you will start thinking of more and more goals, in detail and with exact ideas of how they should be. No goals are too big or too small; if it's what you want, then put it on your list. Often small goals will get you a few steps closer to your larger goals, and that's the best way to achieve them, by going step by step.

You can write a list of what you don't want, and often this is easier as we all know what we don't like or are unhappy with. We are often so focused on this that we don't even know what we want. By writing down what we don't want, we can look at each point individually and think of our ideal opposite. Many people find that by doing this, they realise what they are missing in their lives; this could be their current situation or failures. Instead of focusing on them as a victim, we take each one and think of what we would like instead. There you will have a list of wants and therefore, a list of goals. So many times, people are unhappy with their lives, unsatisfied and looking for more; write those things down. What are the things you dislike and why? Now take each item on your list and really take a moment to think about them. Why is it like that? What is the opposite or ideal situation? What would you like instead? Is it possible to turn this situation around? Is a new situation necessary? Is it a limiting belief or fear that is causing this situation, or is it something you need to work towards? Break down each and every dislike until you get to the like.

You can create a vision board or book, and stick pictures in it of everything you would like. I usually find these are not as effective as the previous two methods as it does not go into the specific details of defining each goal and really taking the time to process each goal. However, it can be used as an incentive or starting point and help keep your goals in your focus.

Sometimes when we progress in life towards what we want, we realise we don't, in fact, want the same things anymore and have to adjust our goals to match our current perspectives. We often change our beliefs of what we want and need out of life with personal growth. Usually we start out looking for material gain and superficial wants or needs and as we progress find these things are no longer important to us, leading us to look for and achieve more challenging and substantial goals which can reward us in more meaningful ways.

MAINTAINING YOUR GOALS

Once you have your goal, have a plan in place and a strategy for obtaining it, the next thing to do is constantly maintain your focus on getting to your goal. Many people create lists of goals, and come up with all sorts of plans and then never do anything about them. They get distracted, they get busy with their everyday lives, their home or family life takes over, and the list goes on. There is no point in making changes in our lives, working out what we want out of life and creating plans if we are never going to do anything about them.

Create smaller goals within your main goal - small steps which can bring you closer to achieving what you want. These small achievements will keep you motivated as well. By breaking up the goal into smaller steps, you will usually find that it is more easily attainable; it is reasonable and achievable without putting you under enormous or overwhelming pressure.

One of the first things to do, if you do not already have someone helping you plan out your goals - a coach or therapist or friend - is to find someone who will hold you accountable. It is usually better to get someone who is not emotionally involved, invested, or biased in any way. It is less likely that you will give up on your goal when you know there will be someone checking up on you. A coach or therapist is always a better option as they will have the experience necessary to help and guide you throughout your journey. You may find a willing mentor or possibly have multiple people with different insights and knowledge over different areas who can keep you on the right track. Invest in surrounding yourself with people who will support you and who can influence you in a positive and productive way.

The next step would be to look into acquiring any further skills or knowledge that could benefit you in reaching your goal, in taking you past your goal or which can in some way help you to become more productive on your way to achieving what it is you are after. You can never have too much knowledge and you can never ever lose from learning more. The more you learn and understand, the better you can make insightful decisions and possibly achieve greater outcomes.

Practice. Put in the work. You need to be passionate about what you want in order to achieve it. The more you put in, the more you get out.

Evaluate the process. Is it going smoothly? Is it an up-and-down road? Have you met any obstacles, or are there any problems in your plan? Is there anything that needs to be thought out and planned differently to get you to where you want to be? Is something not working out? If so, then why? How can it be changed or made better or easier? Do you need further help or assistance? Can you find a different way?

It is very rare that any goal is achieved without a few obstacles along the way. Instead of seeing them as a failure; look at them as a way to refine your plan, create a better plan and motivate you to find alternative ways in which to get where you want to be. There is always a way if you know how to look.

Hopefully, through reading this book, you have gained some insight as to why change and taking responsibility for our lives is so important, and you have a clearer idea of why understanding our body and its processes, listening to our bodies and having the awareness of symptoms from our body's response to how we live our lives; have a significant impact on our life's experience. That, understanding our perceptions and behaviours has a direct impact on everything we do on a daily basis, on how we feel and in turn affect on our physical bodies as well. We all live our lives wanting positive outcomes, yet we need to make the right choices both mentally and physically in order to achieve this. By using the ideas and principles in this book, it is possible to live a healthier, more productive life and, as such, be rewarded with a greater future ahead of us.

Or could this all be; nothing more than just another perspective...

NOTES AND REFERENCES

Acharya S & Shukla S. (2012). P.118 Mirror neurons: Enigma of the metaphysical Modular brain. Journal of Natural Sciences and Biological Medicine. 3(2):118-24.

Furnham, A (2020). Psychology 101, London. Bloomsbury Business Publishing.

Sundberg, Taplin, Tyler (1983). Introduction to clinical psychology - perspectives, issues, and contributions to human service, New Jersey. Prentice-Hall

Hewstone, M; Stroebe, W; Codol,JP; Stephenson, G (1988). Great Britain. University Press, Cambridge.

Busch, C (2020). The Serendipity Mindset, Great Britain. Penguin Random House.

Canfield, J (2017). How to get from where you are to where you want to be, Great Britain. Thorsons.

Van Der Kolk, B (2014). The body keeps score, Great Britain. Penguin Random House.

Duffy, B (2019). The perils of perception- why we're wrong about nearly everything, London. Atlantic Books.

Dias, D (2017). The ten types of human, Great Britain. Penguin Random House.

Scott Peck, M (1990). The road less travelled, Great Britain: Arrow Books. First published Hutchinson & Co. Great Britain: 1983.

Freud, A (1937). The Ego and the mechanism of Defence, London. Hogarth Press and Institute of Psycho-Analysis.

Gentry, J. Eric. (2021)Treating Complex PTSD, Forward Facing Institute: Complet PTSD Healing Trauma: Simple Not Easy, Udemy training course. CPTSD Training Manual (2021).

McLeod, S. A. (2009). DefenceMechanisms, www.simplypsychology.org/defence-mechanisms.

Leaf, C (2021). How are the mind and brain different, www.mindbodygreen.com

Freud, S (1894). The Neuro-psychosis of defence, SE, 3: 41-61.

Freud, S (1896). Further remarks on the Neuro-psychosis of defence, SE, 3: 157-184.

Freud, S (1933). New introductory lectures on psychoanalysis. London: Hogarth Press and institute of psychoanalysis, Pp. xi +240.

Turney, J (2018) Cracking Neuroscience, Great Britain. Octopus Puublishing Group

Krishnagopal, D (2014). The biology of thought, United States Academic Press.

All definitions are sourced from the Oxford Languages, https://languages.oup.com/research/oxford-english-dictionary/

Neuroscience and Neuroanatomy references sourced and studied from - DR Najeeb, https://www.drnajeeblectures.com/ :Master Neuroscience and Neuroanatomy Course.

ABOUT THE AUTHOR

Christina Andrianatos is a Professional Counsellor, Psychotherapist and Master's Certified Life Coach with Diplomas of Excellence in Neuroscience and Neuroanatomy as well as Modern Applied Psychology, specialising in NeuroLinguistic NLP programming, as well as being a Certified Cognitive Behavioural Therapist and PTSD Specialist Counsellor, Nutrition and Health Coach. Christina is currently studying towards her Doctorate of Psychology. Her research began with her passion for the human mind, personality theories and healthy mind – healthy body principles, and her own experience and work in trauma victim research and therapy.

www.ingramcontent.com/pod-product-compliance
Lightning Source LLC
Chambersburg PA
CBHW062104270326
41931CB00013B/3200